LIKE

WATER

IAIN QUINTYNE

LIKE WATER

ISBN: 0578400782
ISBN-13: 9780578400785

I FOUND YOU, NOW WHAT?

I haven't felt this way in a long time. I feel as if something has awakened within me; as if the universe is saying, this is my purpose. This is why I am here. I need this, but **someone else needs my words more than I do.**

Passion, for me, is what keeps me up at night. It is what scares me into the fetal position. You know, the "thing" in the back of your mind or corner of your heart that's always there? That's my passion. It took me awhile to listen to that "thing." I was too busy paying attention to my fear; fear of failure. The fear that says, "What if they don't like it? What if I'm not as good as I think I am?" But then came, **"What if I win at this?"**

I became frustrated with always searching externally for my **purpose**. You see, my purpose has to be synonymous with my passion. This is the way my mind works. One day I decided to look internally. I started to realize that I had been running from my own demands for too long. I wasn't putting my **energy** in the right places. I said, "Self, what are your natural abilities? What are those things that fulfill you?" From that inner dialogue came, *Like Water.*

Like Water, is my **heart and head** attempting to make peace with one another. It is me in my entirety; the part of me that I have never whispered to a soul; the part of me that some know all too well. *Like Water,* is **my therapy, my healing, and self-realization**. I hope it can be the catalyst in yours as well. Thank you, and I hope you enjoy the journey.

AFFIRMATIONS

Know Your Worth

Learn to love yourself separately from anyone else,

For love of self speaks unheard volumes to everyone else.

Letting Go

Be the person you were before the world sank its teeth into you.

It's ok to let go of the things that don't feed your soul.

What You Make It

Time isn't flying.

We just aren't doing things worth slowing down for.

Sense of Self

She was whole when they met,

He was her compliment—

Nothing more,

Nothing less—

No societal constraints,

No expectations set.

She was whole when they met.

Beginning of the End

Saving you from yourself was the kindest gesture I could make;

Words from your heart told me it was there for me to take.

Selfish, but why can't we live our wildest dreams?

Actions not intentions are the keys we use

To unlock levels where we've never been;

Scared to make a move and trying not to sin,

Saving you from yourself, is how our story ends.

Be Patient ——It Will Come

Completely open to thoughts that were never spoken

Cold shoulders turn into strangers that were never open

Consistency is the unwritten rule of those that were chosen

Chances came second nature to those that never folded

Karma came back to the ones that distorted the story as they
told it

Pride fell upon those that felt the need to never show it

Emotions came to the ones that didn't know how to hold it

Patience came to those who in silence always spoke it.

Can You See Me?

What if actors really weren't acting and

they played themselves?

How could you judge a book by its cover when it

has two sides,

Even when it's on the shelf?

When your story's over, will they say you played yourself?

Built up others but you made yourself,

Proof to others matters less than proof to self.

A Dish Best Served Cold

Who are you really?

Who do you want to become?

If I showed you who I really was, would you want to run?

I can't say that this is easy, and I can tell you're numb.

I stopped feeling years ago, and I should've told you then,

Everything you meant to me I buried deep within.

I stopped needing long ago as I plotted my revenge—

Revenge for a heart like mine that started off as pure,

Slowly I was tainted, and my pure heart was no more.

So now I have no regrets as the world will come to see,

Toxic hearts and tainted words—revenge for someone

like me.

Alone

What I have always known:

Not good enough in other's eyes

Barely there in my own

Looking for acceptance,

Instead of working on what's inside

Trying to prove myself wrong

Never fit in or out of the box

Never felt like I belong

No greater pain than the feeling of being alone—

This is what I have always known.

LIKE WATER

The Birds

You barely even notice we watch you all the day.
We watched you as you birthed a nation.

We watch when you are kind,
We watch you when you hate,
We watch with much dismay.

We know you came from greatness for we have traveled to
your land.
We know it's hard to see the light when darkness

clouds your path.

We watch you as you make it, even if the odds are stacked.
We watch you as you stumble but choose to

keep coming back.

Your journey is far from over, it will be hard and hopeless, at
least to you, it seems.

We'll watch you as your past glory returns. All is right in the
world it will seem.

Guardians

Watch over me while I sleep,

Please say something before I weep,

Please rescue me before it gets too deep.

They say that life is in the eyes.

The only way to tell the truth is to shield it from the lies.

Getting better at ending things with no closure needed.

Felt my way through the maze before I could see it.

Alarm at the Gate

A trillion worth of spending power and economically unaware.

I don't even know who I am, so why should I care?

A house divided falls and I guess that was the point.

No access to real wealth, so I'm in this for self.

Then you ask me, "Why can't I be satisfied?"

Like my freedom was enough but even that was the saddest lie.

Then you ask, "Why do you use drugs to get high?"

Then I reply, "You use the same drugs, but your privilege is different than I."

The better question is, "How can we sit back and watch our people die?"

You reply, "Yes, it's sad, but it's not our lives."

What Dreams are Made Of

But did I fly too high?

Maybe I flew too close.

The heat was relief to know that I could never dream too low.

My heart can't take it.

Please forgive me if I was too impatient.

On the wings of my dreams, I just had to make it.

Feeling out of my element, but I just can't face it;

When who I see isn't a reflection of what the world

sees in me.

Regrets

Someone's stealing time

Without any reason or rhyme.

There's no feeling more sublime than to have all of my time.

I'm here to report a crime—someone's stealing time!

You see these wrinkles and these lines? There's no way they can be mine.

Someone's stealing time.

If I could have some back, that would be fine;

Just a little more and I promise not to whine.

Someone's stealing time.

Learn from Y(OUR) Mistakes

How do I start at the beginning when it hurts too much?

People watching at school when we used to laugh so much

I remember telling my roommate that all I wanted was her.

After all the crying, all I wanted was out.

I guess that's the reality, when neither of us loved

ourselves that much.

Too immature to admit that I failed you in many ways;

Surprised that we stuck it out for so many days.

You last came to me in a dream and it was like our first date.

Take things for granted no more; I learned from our fate

Broken

Where would I be if I was my heart?

How would I heal if I was my heart?

Should I continue to beat if I was my heart?

The end comes at some point, no matter the start.

Face It; It's Over

Please stop acting like things haven't changed.

If you say you love me too, I'll devote myself to you.

But I don't know us anymore,

I guess I barely knew you.

Now I'm crying in the shower,

Wishing you would take this pain away.

If this ends the way I think it will,

Please don't judge all relationships,

Just know we gave our all for this.

Transparency

Do you even see me?

Can you tell that I'm there?

Does my whisper haunt you?

Do you even hear?

Can't you see I need you?

Can't you see I care?

You don't even see me;

You can't tell I'm here.

Acceptance of Self

I thought I could be everything to everyone,

Until I realized that the only expectations that weren't met,

were mine.

Why can't I just accept that perfection is not reality?

I want things I don't need, but those things want me.

Addicted to buying, but selling my self-worth in actuality.

Lost and Found

I gasped for air and found none.

I guess the weight was too much.

They tell me I should feel this way instead, but I can't

Relate too much.

Confessions over Jack, I hope I don't drink too much.

The worst of me came at the best of times

Without consequences the night that I changed my life;

Redemption comes in the dark in the form of light.

I Never Stood a Chance

Why does it seem like they always leave when you

Need them the most?

Was I not worth the struggle?

Could your time have been better spent?

In life there are choices—I guess it wasn't me you chose.

The Ego Knows Too Much

We went places we said we never would.

Love became mundane, and I thought we said that it

never should.

I know you said some things that my pride couldn't handle—

You know I said some things that you should never stand for.

Pride before the fall no more, true statement of fact.

When my ego fell, how was I supposed to react?

LIKE WATER

Fin.

Our love can't be over; I'm still lost in it.

Went off the deep end and I got caught in it.

Tell me, what are we to do when the feelings aren't there,

and the tears multiply as we divide our affairs?

What do I tell your friends when they call in disbelief?

Thought we were set in stone, but the wedding talks ceased.

I hope you're happy now.

I hope I'll be happy now.

Anxiety and Destiny

Everything's moving faster than I can think.

Palms sweaty as I rush to the bathroom sink;

I can hear you but I don't understand.

I'm not ready for this and how dare you think I am.

Pretty sure I didn't ask for this,

And to think this all started from a kiss.

Your secrets are no longer yours to keep.

You transferred all of you to me;

Intertwined in bliss so sweet in the end our souls will meet.

LIKE WATER

Dear My Broken Heart,

Why I am this way you say you don't understand.

Hard to trust what we have between us. I'm so scarred.

Been hurt a million times and it's always the same song.

If you weren't ready, why'd you come knocking at my door?

Remember, diligence to our feelings teaches us healing.

Understanding comes from hurt, and to trust our feelings.

Mistakes are not exclusive and neither are lessons

learned in lust.

Every page torn from our love story, reminds me still to trust.

For after dawn must come dusk.

Opaque

I can let you see all my sins.

Thankless favors you won't see,

At this point you have all of me.

Disappearing into the wind, I guess that's the lesson

I had to learn,

I guess that's why we let it burn.

Ashes to ashes in the urn, I can't tell if I'm still hurt;

I guess that's why we make it worse.

We make it so you'll never forget our name.

You'll curse the day my tears came down like rain.

Best Wishes

Everything I could live without—

Without my fears,

Without my doubt.

When I think about you, do you think about me?

Life is just a reflection of things we want it to be;

Reset and then you'll start close to me.

Everything I thought for you, it was supposed to be.

She calls me man and I call her she.

Everything I want for you so it shall be.

Jaded

Lived your life now a thousand times.

I've come up with a thousand lies.

When shallow hearts conceive with shallow minds,

Energy releases as legs divide.

The world corrupts it always has

Religion for peace of mind — a fair trade indeed

Everyone still searching for their own inner peace.

Stay

Do you know what it takes to be free?

It takes a life not meant to be,

A life in which you feel,

A life in which you allow yourself to heal.

If you knew what it took to live this life would you

give it away?

I hope I've convinced you it's worth it, so please stay.

Fallen

Later means bye these days.

Lies come during dates.

People can alter their fate.

Made up my mind we'll never meet again.

I guess we made up our minds, we'll never speak again.

Mountains will crumble and stars will fall,

Does it mean there's no forever in anything at all?

Unplug

I was never meant for any of this,

It's more apparent day by day,

My skin crawls as I try to submit,

Fear kills off hope as I try to resist.

Breaking into pieces and then picking them up,

Breaking out my mind when enough is enough.

I can't feel anymore, I'm just so numb.

Run, run, run from the life I didn't love.

The Heart is Fickle

Through all my plights and my falls, I still follow my call.

Through my highs and my ups, through my lows when I fall,

You tell me you love me but I'm not ready at all.

You keep leaving me messages, I keep ignoring your calls.

No I don't hate you I'm so confused at it all.

I don't love myself,

I can't love you at all.

Mirror, mirror

You were me before I became you,

If you looked deep inside, you would realize it's true.

A lot of love to give but regrets still linger,

So now you're more cautious with whom you give

your heart to.

I can't change the past but I wouldn't want to

Because you were me before I became you.

Late Nights are for Wallowing

Staying in drinking alone just because it feels good.

Unprotected everything just because it feels good.

My decisions only hurt me, is what I think to make

me feel good.

My insecurities make me feel numb, and in reality,

my above decisions

When sober, make me feel dumb.

I wrestle with reality and question it all.

Who's there to catch us if we never fall?

Fallen from grace, that's what forgiveness is for.

Forgive, but not forget, that's what vengeance is for.

The Vibes are Off

Too much faith in you and too much emotion.

Too little faith in the process, and the direction I am going.

Too much attention that I need and maybe that's my flaw.

Too little evidence that you care and maybe that's my sign.

A sign of things, of things to come, all revealed in time.

Apologies While Sitting Alone

I am not sure how this works, but if it was, then it should.

Don't know if your heart still beats for me, but if it did,

then it could.

When I said those things, I was hurt;

What I really meant, is that I love you too much and

myself so little.

Your worth was never mine to evaluate.

Your actions were never mine to hate.

I'm sorry.

Learn to Pick Yourself Up

Failed because you chose to never try again

Rock bottom because you chose to never fly again

Prideful because you chose to never hurt again

Shy because you chose to never flirt again

Smiled because you chose to never cry again

Confident because you chose to never be defined again

Spoke the truth because you chose to never lie again.

It'll Be Better Once You Wake

All of my time and my effort never impressed you.

With a list of excuses for you, I came back each time.

In the end, you'll say, "But we can be friends."

When you kissed me, the world lit up; you felt it too.

I want you to be happy even if we don't speak.

Life has a sick sense of humor, don't you find?

Woke up from this nightmare, just to find

You're right here next to me. It was all in my mind.

The Promise

You must actively pursue happiness in order to have it, and you must decide that you are going to be happy, despite less than ideal circumstances. For like most things, happiness must be nurtured and guarded at all times.

Insecurity

Not sure I've ever been in love and that's real.

Sorry to those who loved me, but that's how I feel.

Always one moment away from happiness;

Self-sabotage at its finest, but I felt you deserved more.

Surreal moments together forever is what you lived for.

Someone else's now, and I have myself to blame.

Insecurities ran wild through my mind,

Arguing about the same things we argued about last night.

Maybe in some ways, you should thank me;

I got you away from me;

The destroyer of all good things eventually.

Meet in the Middle

No two people arrive at love using the same way.

The trick is to love that person in the way they want to be

loved because you know that they will give you the type of

love you desire in return.

That's compromise.

Arguments about Nothing

Falling out of love with my decision making,

I can't even tell you what a toll it has taken.

Should I pick it up or should I put it down?

Conscience telling me that I'm in trouble now.

Picking up the pieces but they keep on breaking.

Brain is telling me that my heart can't take it.

Tell me what you do when your faith is broken.

Tell me how to make it go away.

With every empty second my heart starts to race.

Where you at? What you doing?

My thoughts start to pace back and forth in my head.

Overreact, that's it! Start a fight!

Threaten to end it!

Guarded hearts never break free,

Broken hearts seem to find me.

LIKE WATER

Searching

In between my feelings is where you'll find me,

Never far from you, but never really there—

Distant even when I'm near.

I was never easy. I think I've spent too much time alone.

Where do you run to when you call nowhere home?

The Theory of Opportunity

We ask for things we think we want, but we are not truly ready to receive them. To see if we're actually ready for what we're asking, the universe will put exactly what we ask for, within reach.

If we choose to do nothing with this opportunity, we are met with some form of disappointment. Don't waste opportunities and time, thinking that if it's for you, it will be. Effort is rewarded, not complacency.

Waiting on You to Arrive

I have things but they don't mean anything to me.

They are masks for my insecurities,

Giving it all to people who've earned nothing.

Never asked for much, just wanted you to do something

Before the night fades and darkness turns to day.

All light to those whose heart never shied away.

Find Yourself

I have a feeling this isn't who I'm supposed to be.

Without foundation, a structure will lack identity.

Naïve to think happy endings were meant to be;

Maybe they were for some, but not sure about me.

I have an inkling this isn't who I'm supposed to be.

Where Did We Go Wrong?

The illusion of materiality is that from the outside looking in,
it looks stable.

But true wealth, lies in the mind, heart and spirit. This is truly
the essence of human capital.

It All Feels Wrong

My expectations for you were too high.

Can you blame my heart for being addicted to you

night after night?

Fixed in my position and stuck in my ways.

Love can't be a drug because I'm dying for it to go away.

You were a girl that was my world and you shined like a pearl.

I guess we shun the ones that love us and forgive the ones

that don't need us.

Deep down we're all the same,

Lusting for all the wrong things.

What's a life lived if you made all the same mistakes?

Prince of the Fall

Can you match my mood on a fall night?

Can I watch as you fall in love on a fall night?

Explicit wishes turn into deep kisses.

In and out of your soul with every breath.

Can you tell I studied every inch of you for this test?

Tell me that you know what this is and that at this moment,

I can fulfill your every wish.

Each touch means a little more;

Feel me as I go deep enough to reach your core,

Tell me that you want more.

Every inch is what you fought for.

Sins of the Father

I feel so much was taken,

I'm so scared to take it back;

Scared of my emotions right now,

Scared to fade to black.

How could I pay for his decisions?

How did we lose it all at once?

Years passed and we grew older,

Regretting each passing month.

My pride can't say I'm hurting.

My pride can't say I'm broken,

Can't say I wish that things were different,

Can't miss what I never had.

If I could say just one thing,

I'd say I miss having a dad.

False Evidence

Too much goes unsaid.

Am I free to cave under the pressure of my reality?

Sometimes I'm a victim of my dreams,

Held hostage by not knowing what's meant for me,

Terrified to try with nothing to lose;

Except I can lose my anxiety,

I can lose my fear of failure—

No longer am I lost then.

Potential turned to reality,

This is what I was meant to be.

No more nights numbing myself scared to clock in.

Never going back only forward steps.

20s

Sleep on couches

Find out who your real friends are

Don't apologize for being yourself

Think for yourself

Let them see you're hurt

See and feel your joy

Excited because the day holds so much in store

Working on yourself because life disguises no flaws

Take ownership of your life and know it's not all about you

It was one wild ride, but you made it through.

Us

Unlocked from the inside,

Your eyes were the keys to my soul.

If you'll have me, I'll never leave;

I'll make this our home.

I'll leave with a kiss and return later for more.

Years from now, we'll tell our kids how mommy and

daddy met,

"Our souls fell in love and never let go —

A promise made to be kept."

LIKE WATER

It's Not You, it's Me.

I chose you because I feared receiving the love I

wanted most.

Even in the times I held you close, I knew.

When I smiled at the thought of you, I knew.

Over and over I punished myself.

Maturity doesn't come with age, it comes with

finding yourself.

It was the best of me and the worst of me,

Yet, at my best, I drank from your well thirstily.

At my worst I over-indulged in your company.

For what it's worth, I needed you more than you

needed me.

I wanted broken, and I got it in the form of me.

Creatures of the Night

Nights bring out the best in us,

All of our dreams come true.

Nights bring out the best in us,

I hope it brings it out of you,

I hope you can feel it too.

I can't always tell wrong from right,

I don't know how to live in light.

When the sun goes down and my interest peaks;

It's time to go wild and live in the night.

LIKE WATER

Pennies in the Well

If I had all of the change in a wishing well.

For all of the times someone wished me well,

And for every time those prayers fell,

On deaf ears; oh how they fell.

Out of touch with reality, and I don't mind too much.

We came from the heavens so in our faith we trust.

As shallow as I am I can't seem to stay afloat,

I can't help but to keep thinking we reap what we sow.

I'd be lying if I said I don't think about what's next.

The meaning of this life and everything that comes with it,

The meaning of a kiss and the innocence that goes with it,

The meaning of, "I love you," and the promises

it leaves behind.

Pain Yields Growth

The void that was left could never be filled by nice things.

It could only be filled by the wisdom that pain brings.

Better to Have Loved

The divide between us, became too wide, to close.

The hurt we shared, took us to places we shouldn't go.

I was naïve to think my hope could change us.

I guess you couldn't help yourself, you were stuck

in your ways.

Oh how I dreamed of better days,

Oh how I yearned for better ways

To communicate

Tears in my eyes, as I lay awake at night.

Why fight for something that's broken between two adults?

Why lie, I knew happiness wasn't here?

I only held on for fear of missing out,

Handicapped by the same cheers that rang out when we

hit it off.

This is it how it feels to have loved and lost.

Lies on the Inside

I have plenty demons, Love.

I'm not as found as you think.

Mercy me I'm too far gone,

I could disappear in a blink.

I dream in shades of grey and black;

You dream in shades of pink.

Your light was first to give me life.

Moment's fleet and skies turn bleak;

Debauchery runs the night.

LIKE WATER

Tears from St. Joseph

Guilty of not being the person I told myself to be.

Life was moving fast and I didn't try to stop it.

Then you were called away, and I knew that I had lost it.

Time is of the essence, and to forget that can prove costly.

Part of me died that day, and I'm afraid that I deserved it.

I miss everything about you, yet took it all for granted.

I pray that you knew my heart and that I tried to plan it.

When regret is what precedes your tears, it's

hard to even stand up.

The moral here, is take nothing in this life for granted.

Wishful Thinking

Sick and tired of being sick and tired.

Wish for once I could be the admired and not the admirer.

Wish that I could be more than an afterthought.

Wish I was as important to you as you are to yourself.

Wish I didn't feel so selfish for looking after myself.

Deserving of more, I played your fool for the last time.

The only wish I have now, is that I wish you a safe good-bye.

Ripples

All the bridges are now burnt.

My, how I miss those places I used to go —

Those places I still know —

Reminded of a time in life I reaped, but did not sow.

Ripples in time are all we are,

Imperfect souls searching for peace.

The Illusion

Ass backwards in how we go about getting what we want,

Saying you want commitment, but too afraid to be alone.

So you settle in and forget who you are just to get burned.

Superficial in all things you say you want.

Can't you see true happiness lies within self?

Not cars,

Not clothes,

Not in anyone else,

Not in your addictions that you hide so well,

Not in any of the shit you buy so well.

Oh well, I guess only time will tell.

The Author of Your Pain

When I pulled the last straw, that was all she wrote,

Even though she was the author of all my hope.

On my ninth life, and I still haven't found myself.

She could save me, but where's the fun in that?

A woman in all of her glory through and through.

They told me she was meant for more than a leech like you.

I died that night on the kitchen floor.

She had no more chapters to write; no more hope to implore.

It Will Come

Decisions being made that question our integrity.

How would you act if I told you, you were a king or queen?

Is there anybody out there waiting for someone like me?

I don't want to play the old games,

In fact, I'm already in a different league.

Making the same mistakes, I guess that's insanity.

My persistence with perfection, points to my deficiencies.

You see, security comes with flaws, and with knowing

I'm a rarity.

Can you help me fix my mind, so that it's only my

third eye that's allowed to see?

Haunted

What could have been is haunting.

For what lies, come from failure, and what truths

come from death?

The beauty of it all, is that you get to walk away.

Find the beauty in your sorrow, and the happiness

in your pain.

The more green the grass, the more it needs the rain.

The more things change, the more they stay the same.

"What if I fail," said no one destined to be great?

No man or woman is a slave to their own fate.

LIKE WATER

We, the Blind Mice

Why do none of the systems in place prepare us to survive?

Instead they prepare us to take orders everyday of our lives;

Instead of making "free" slaves, I wish they

pushed independence.

But then again, who would push their twisted agendas?

Break the cycle of needless consumption,

Only plunging us deeper into debt, and at the

mercy of corporations.

There's more to life than having the finer things,

Falling into the traps that money and fame bring.

Learn how to love your fellow man,

Respect the woman that prays,

Take care of one another.

I hope this reaches you in time.

I know that all wounds heal in time.

Enough

I've lost too many things I wish that I could get back.

More often than not, the kind of love I give, is

never given back.

Seems like a trap, but let me explain that:

The biggest hearts are often broken with no one to

heal it back,

Loving you like you're the only other person on Earth.

The depth of your oceans only leave me submersed.

Yes, I can see it, but can you see your own worth?

I guess we can be secrets to ourselves, when we're dealing

with too much hurt.

Enough (cont.)

How could you stay the same? That's not what life is
supposed to be.

So when I tell them who I was, how dare any of them judge;

Like when everything came down around, they were there

to pick me up.

The messes that we make of our lives, do we dare to

clean them up?

I knew that you were hurting, yet I still signed up;

Gave comfort to your worries,

Listened to your stories,

Until you became enough.

"Am I really good enough?"

"Live your dreams or someone else will."

"When you fail to try, you truly have lost it all."

These were my daily thoughts. I failed to launch so many times before because of False Evidence Appearing Real. My potential was drowning in a sea of doubt. My message to you is, SEIZE IT ALL! I started writing my story when I decided to write, *Like Water*. I implore you to do the same. The time we have is short, and it cannot be wasted living someone else's dream.

I hope that this book has helped you as much as it has helped me. Writing wasn't always in my plan, but all of this had to come out. I feel that communication, empathy and love without condition, can solve most of the problems we face in the world today. This is my first attempt at leaving the world a better place than I found it.

Thank you.